|| Dedicated to all wisdom seekers around the World ||

SECRETS TO MOTIVATE YOURSELF FOR SUCCESS

STRATEGIES FOR REACHING YOUR GOALS

DR. JAGADEESH PILLAI

Made with ❤ on the Notion Press Platform
www.notionpress.com

Contents

Contents

PRAYER

"Om Bhadram Karnebhih Shrunuyaama DevaahBhadram Pashyemaakshabhiryajatraah SthiraiirangaistushtuvaamsastanoobhihVyashema Devahitam YadaayuhSwasti Na Indro VridhashravaahSwasti Nah Pooshaa VishwavedaahSwasti Nastaarkshyo ArishtanemihSwasti No Brihaspatir DadhaatuOm Shantih, Shantih, Shantih"

The literal meaning of this mantra is: OM. O Gods! Let us hear auspicious words from our ears. O reverent Gods! Let us behold propitious visions from our eyes, let our organs and body be stable, healthy, and strong. Let us do that which is pleasing to the gods in the life span allotted to us. May Indra, inscribed in the scriptures, bring us fortune! May Pushan, the knower of the world, grant us prosperity! May Trakshya, who vanquishes enemies, bestow us with blessings! May Brihaspati bring us success!
OM Peace, Peace, Peace.

About The Author

Dr. Jagadeesh Pillai is a renowned Guinness World Record holder, writer, and researcher hailing from Varanasi, also known as the abode of Lord Shiva. With a Ph.D. in Vedic Science and a range of creative ideas and achievements, he is a true polymath. He is the author of more than 100 books including Research Publications. Although his roots can be traced back to Kerala, the people of Varanasi hold him in high regard and affectionately consider him one of their own.

In 1998, Dr. Pillai was offered a job at Banaras Hindu University, but he left the position after only two months to pursue greater goals in life. He believed that in order to study Indian scriptures and engage in other creative endeavours, he needed to retire from the daily grind of working solely for money at a young age.

He started an export business from scratch, using the knowledge he had gained from a previous job in the industry. His intelligence and unique approach to business led to great success in a short period of time, earning him more in just a decade and a half than he would have in a lifetime working in a government job. Upon the passing of Dr. APJ Abdul Kalam, Dr. Pillai decided to leave the business and dedicate himself to reading, studying, researching, and experimenting.

During his tenure in the export business, Dr. Pillai traveled to over 16 countries, gaining valuable insight and experiencing the world and life in detail.

Dr. Pillai has achieved four Guinness World Records in the following subjects:

"Script to Screen" - In this record, Dr. Pillai produced and directed an animation film within the shortest time possible, breaking the previous record set by Canadians. He has also received numerous national and international awards and recognitions for this achievement.

Longest Line of Postcards - For this record, Dr. Pillai created a line of 16,300 postcards on the occasion of the 163rd anniversary of Indian Postal Day. The event also included a questionnaire about the Indian flag.

Largest Poster Awareness Campaign - Dr. Pillai designed an awareness campaign on the subject of "Beti Bachao - Beti Padhao" (Save the Girl Child - Educate the Girl Child) to achieve this record.

Largest Envelope - In tribute to the Indian Prime Minister's "Make in India" initiative, Dr. Pillai created a 4000 square meter envelope using waste paper to achieve this record.

Attempted - **70000 Candles on a 210 kg Cake** - To celebrate the 70th Indian Independence Day, Dr. Pillai attempted to light 70,000 candles on a 210 kg cake, which was recorded in World Records India.

Attempted - **Documentary on Dhamek Stupa of Sarnath in 17 Languages** - Dr. Pillai attempted to create a documentary on the Dhamek Stupa of Sarnath, dubbing it in 17 different languages. The result of this attempt is currently awaiting confirmation from the Guinness World Records.

Dr. Pillai is skilled in teaching the Bhagavad Gita, a Hindu scripture, and is popular among young people. He has helped many young people improve their lives through his motivational teachings.

In addition to teaching, he has composed and sung numerous Sanskrit Bhajans and patriotic songs.

He has also written and directed several short films and documentaries for awareness campaigns, and has volunteered with the police in both UP and Kerala to spread awareness about various issues through videos and photography.

Incredibly, he has produced and directed over 100 documentaries about the city of Varanasi, all on his own.

He has also helped and guided more than 25 boys and girls to achieve world records through creative and innovative methods. He is a multifaceted person who uses his intellect and the blessings given to him by God to excel in various areas. He is both a teacher and a student, always learning and teaching, and is able to master any subject he comes across.

He is a selfless social activist and motivational speaker who has overcome struggles and failures to become a successful and enthusiastic individual with a rich life experience.

In addition to his work with the Bhagavad Gita, he is also an efficient Tarot card reader, Astro-Vastu consultant, and a talented singer and composer. He has sung the entire Ram Charita Manas and Bhagavad Gita in his own compositions, and has sung the phrase "Lokah Samastha Sukhino Bhavantu" in 50 different languages. He is currently working on a detailed and scientific study of Vedas, Upanishads, Puranas, and the Bhagavad Gita. He has also composed and sung the Hanuman Chalisa and Gayatri Mantra in 108 and 1008 different compositions, respectively.

Awards - Four Times Guinness World Records, Winner of Mahatma Gandhi Vishwa Shanti Puraskar, Mahatma Gandhi Global Peace Ambassador, Kashi Ratna Award, Dr. APJ Abdul Kalam Motivational Person of the Year 2017, Mother Teresa Award, Indira Gandhi Priyadarshini Award, Bharat Vikas Ratna Award, Udyog Ratna Award, Vigyan Prasar Award, Poorvanchal Ratn Samman.

Preface

"Secrets to Motivate Yourself for Success Strategies for Reaching Your Goals" is a comprehensive guide to self-motivation, designed to help you reach your full potential and achieve your goals. In this book, you will learn practical and actionable strategies to cultivate and sustain self-motivation, overcome obstacles, and achieve success.

Self-motivation is the driving force behind all personal and professional growth, and it is the key to unlocking your potential and reaching your goals. Whether you are looking to advance your career, improve your relationships, or simply lead a more fulfilling life, self-motivation is the foundation upon which all progress is built.

In this book, you will learn about the psychology of self-motivation and the importance of setting SMART goals, creating a plan, building a daily routine, overcoming procrastination and staying focused, building mental and physical resilience, managing negative emotions, building self-esteem through positive affirmations, the power of positive thinking and gratitude, dealing with failure and learning from mistakes, building a support system and connecting with others, finding and pursuing your passions, understanding and managing perfectionism, building self-compassion, and the role of mindfulness in self-motivation.

With practical and actionable advice, and real-life examples to illustrate each principle, this book provides a roadmap to help you achieve your goals with self-motivation and reach new heights of personal and professional success.

So, let's dive into the world of self-motivation and discover the secrets to success!

I

Introduction: Understanding Self-Motivation and its Importance for Success

Self-motivation is a crucial aspect of achieving success in all areas of life. It refers to the drive and determination that comes from within and propels individuals to take action towards their goals. Without self-motivation, even the most well-laid plans and aspirations can remain unfulfilled. In this chapter, we will delve into what self-motivation is, why it is important for success, and how it can be developed and cultivated.

Self-motivation can be defined as the drive and energy that

individuals possess to take action and pursue their goals, without external influence or incentives. It is the fuel that keeps individuals motivated and focused, even when faced with obstacles and setbacks. Self-motivated individuals are driven by their own goals and desires, rather than relying on external rewards or recognition.

The importance of self-motivation for success cannot be overstated. Without it, individuals may struggle to stay committed to their goals and pursue their aspirations. Self-motivation provides the drive and determination necessary to overcome challenges and persist in the face of difficulties. It is the foundation of personal growth and development and enables individuals to reach their full potential.

Self-motivation can be developed and cultivated through various methods and strategies. Building a growth mindset, setting achievable goals, creating a supportive environment, and establishing positive habits and routines are just a few ways to boost self-motivation. Additionally, individuals can adopt an attitude of self-reflection, assess their strengths and weaknesses, and continuously work on developing their skills and abilities.

Self-motivation is a critical component of success and personal growth. It provides individuals with the drive and determination to pursue their goals and overcome obstacles. By understanding the importance of self-motivation, individuals can develop and cultivate it, enabling them to reach their full potential and achieve success in all areas of their lives.

In the following chapters, we will explore in detail various strategies and techniques for developing self-motivation, and how to apply these to reach your goals and achieve success.

"Motivation is the art of getting people to do what you want them to do because they want to do it."

- Dwight D. Eisenhower

☙

II

Setting SMART Goals and Creating a Plan

One of the most effective ways to boost self-motivation is by setting well-defined, achievable goals. Setting SMART goals provides a clear roadmap for success and helps individuals focus their efforts on what is most important. In this chapter, we will explore what SMART goals are and how to create a plan for reaching them.

SMART goals are Specific, Measurable, Achievable, Relevant, and Time-bound objectives that individuals set for themselves. These goals provide a clear and concise roadmap for success and ensure that individuals are focused on what is most important.

The first step in setting SMART goals is to be specific. Goals should be clear and concise, with a well-defined outcome in mind. For example, instead of setting a goal to "get in shape," a specific goal would be "to lose 10 pounds in the next three months."

Next, goals should be measurable. This means that individuals should be able to track their progress and determine whether they are on track to reaching their goal. For example, if the goal is to "lose 10 pounds in three months," the individual can measure their progress by tracking their weight loss each week.

Goals should also be achievable. This means that the goal should be challenging but not impossible. Individuals should set goals that are within reach, given their current skills, resources, and circumstances.

Relevance is another important aspect of SMART goals. Goals should align with the individual's values, interests, and overall life objectives. This ensures that individuals are motivated to work towards their goals, as they are meaningful and important to them.

Finally, goals should be time-bound, with a clear deadline for completion. This creates a sense of urgency and ensures that individuals are working towards their goals in a timely and efficient manner.

Once SMART goals have been set, the next step is to create a plan for reaching them. This may involve breaking down the goal into smaller, more manageable steps, and establishing a timeline for each step. It is also important to identify any obstacles or challenges that may arise and to plan for how to overcome them.

Setting SMART goals and creating a plan is a crucial step in boosting self-motivation and reaching success. By setting well-defined, achievable goals, individuals can focus their efforts on what is most important, track their progress, and stay motivated along the way. In the following chapters, we will delve into specific strategies for reaching your SMART goals and achieving success.

"Success is not final, failure is not fatal: It is the courage to continue that counts."

- Winston S. Churchill

ଊ

III

Building a Daily Routine for Self-Motivation

A daily routine is a powerful tool for cultivating self-motivation and reaching success. By establishing a consistent routine, individuals can create structure and stability in their lives, and focus their efforts on what is most important. In this chapter, we will explore the benefits of building a daily routine and provide practical tips for doing so.

Establishing a daily routine provides a sense of structure and stability, which can boost self-motivation and increase productivity. A routine allows individuals to prioritize their tasks and allocate their time and energy more effectively, helping them to stay focused and motivated.

One of the key benefits of a daily routine is that it helps

to eliminate decision fatigue. Decision fatigue refers to the phenomenon where individuals become exhausted and less effective at making decisions as the day progresses. By having a routine in place, individuals can minimize the number of decisions they need to make, freeing up their mental energy to focus on more important tasks.

Creating a daily routine also provides a sense of accomplishment, as individuals can see the progress they are making towards their goals. This can be especially helpful for individuals who are pursuing long-term goals, as it provides a sense of momentum and encourages them to persist.

To build a daily routine, it is important to start by setting clear goals and priorities. This may involve creating a list of the most important tasks for each day, and determining the best time of day to complete them. It is also important to be flexible and adapt the routine as necessary, as life can be unpredictable.

Incorporating physical activity, meditation, and other forms of self-care into the daily routine can also be incredibly beneficial. Exercise can boost energy levels and enhance overall well-being, while meditation can help individuals to reduce stress and improve focus.

Building a daily routine is a powerful tool for cultivating self-motivation and reaching success. By establishing a consistent routine, individuals can create structure and stability in their lives, prioritize their tasks, and stay motivated towards their goals. In the following chapters, we will explore other strategies for self-motivation, including how to cultivate a growth mindset and build a supportive environment.

"The only way to do great work is to love what you do."

- Steve Jobs

☙

IV

Overcoming Procrastination and Staying Focused

Procrastination is a common barrier to success and can have a detrimental impact on self-motivation. When individuals put things off or avoid their responsibilities, they are less likely to reach their goals and may feel frustrated and discouraged. In this chapter, we will explore the reasons behind procrastination and provide practical tips for overcoming it and staying focused.

Procrastination is often rooted in fear of failure, lack of confidence, or an aversion to the task at hand. It is important to understand the underlying causes of procrastination and to address these issues directly. This may involve seeking support from a coach, therapist, or peer, or using tools like visualization and positive self-talk to boost confidence and build resilience.

One of the most effective strategies for overcoming procrastination is to break down large tasks into smaller, more manageable steps. This can help individuals to feel less overwhelmed and to make progress more quickly. It is also helpful to prioritize tasks based on their level of importance and to focus on one task at a time, rather than trying to do everything at once.

Setting realistic and achievable goals is another important step in overcoming procrastination. When individuals set unrealistic or overly ambitious goals, they are more likely to feel discouraged and unmotivated. By setting realistic goals and tracking progress, individuals can stay motivated and make steady progress towards their goals.

Incorporating positive habits and routines into the daily routine can also help to increase focus and reduce procrastination. This may involve establishing a morning routine, taking regular breaks, and creating a comfortable and supportive workspace.

Overcoming procrastination and staying focused is essential for self-motivation and success. By understanding the underlying causes of procrastination, breaking down tasks into smaller steps, setting realistic goals, and incorporating positive habits and routines, individuals can stay motivated and focused, and achieve their goals. In the following chapters, we will delve deeper into specific strategies for self-motivation, including how to cultivate a growth mindset, seek support from others, and maintain balance and well-being.

"Successful and unsuccessful people do not vary greatly in their abilities. They vary in their desires to reach their potential."

- John Maxwell

V

Building Mental and Physical Resilience

Resilience is a key component of self-motivation and success. It refers to the ability to bounce back from setbacks, challenges, and stress, and to maintain a positive and optimistic outlook. In this chapter, we will explore the importance of building mental and physical resilience and provide practical tips for doing so.

Building mental resilience involves developing a growth mindset, a positive outlook, and a sense of perspective. This may involve practicing positive self-talk, reframing negative thoughts, and seeking support from others when necessary. It is also important to cultivate a sense of purpose and meaning, as this can provide a sense of direction and motivation.

Physical resilience is also essential for self-motivation and success. This involves taking care of one's health and well-being, through regular exercise, healthy eating, and adequate rest. It is also important to manage stress, as this can have a negative impact on physical and mental health. This may involve incorporating relaxation techniques into the daily routine, such as meditation or deep breathing, or seeking support from a therapist or counselor when necessary.

Incorporating a variety of activities into the daily routine can also help to build resilience. This may involve pursuing hobbies and interests, connecting with friends and family, and engaging in physical activity or outdoor recreation. These activities can provide a sense of balance and well-being, and can help individuals to maintain their motivation and focus.

Building mental and physical resilience is a crucial component of self-motivation and success. By developing a growth mindset, maintaining a positive outlook, taking care of one's health and well-being, and incorporating a variety of activities into the daily routine, individuals can cultivate resilience and achieve their goals. In the final chapters of this book, we will explore strategies for maintaining self-motivation and reaching success, including how to celebrate accomplishments, seek feedback and support, and stay motivated in the face of adversity.

"The greatest glory in living lies not in never falling, but in rising every time we fall."

- Nelson Mandela

VI

Understanding and Managing Negative Emotions

Negative emotions, such as fear, frustration, and anxiety, can have a detrimental impact on self-motivation and success. In this chapter, we will explore the reasons behind negative emotions and provide practical tips for understanding and managing them.

It is important to recognize that negative emotions are a normal and natural part of the human experience, and that they serve a purpose in helping us to navigate challenges and stress. However, when negative emotions become persistent or overwhelming, they can interfere with our ability to reach our goals and achieve success.

One effective strategy for managing negative emotions is to identify their source. This may involve reflecting on past experiences, exploring unhelpful thoughts and beliefs, or seeking support from a coach, therapist, or peer. Understanding the source of negative emotions can help individuals to address them more effectively and to prevent them from having a negative impact on their motivation and success.

It is also helpful to engage in activities that promote relaxation and stress reduction. This may include exercise, mindfulness and meditation, or creative pursuits. These activities can help to reduce anxiety and frustration, and to increase feelings of well-being and resilience.

Incorporating positive self-talk and visualization into the daily routine can also help to manage negative emotions. By focusing on positive outcomes, individuals can build confidence and resilience, and overcome obstacles more effectively.

Understanding and managing negative emotions is essential for self-motivation and success. By recognizing the source of negative emotions, engaging in activities that promote relaxation and stress reduction, and incorporating positive self-talk and visualization into the daily routine, individuals can manage negative emotions and achieve their goals. In the next chapter, we will delve deeper into specific strategies for maintaining self-motivation, including how to cultivate gratitude, seek feedback and support, and stay motivated in the face of adversity.

"Don't watch the clock; do what it does. Keep going."

- Sam Levenson

ꕥ

VII

Building Self-Esteem through Positive Affirmations

Self-esteem is an essential component of self-motivation and success. It refers to an individual's sense of worth and confidence in their abilities, and it plays a critical role in determining one's motivation and resilience. In this chapter, we will explore the importance of self-esteem and provide practical tips for building it through positive affirmations.

Positive affirmations are powerful statements that are designed to promote feelings of self-worth, confidence, and motivation. They are typically formulated as simple, positive statements that are repeated on a daily basis. For example, a positive affirmation might be ***"I am capable,***

confident, and successful in all that I do," or "I believe in myself and my ability to achieve my goals."

The power of positive affirmations lies in their ability to reframe negative thoughts and beliefs, and to promote feelings of self-esteem and confidence. By repeating these affirmations on a daily basis, individuals can cultivate a growth mindset, and increase their motivation and resilience in the face of challenges and adversity.

Incorporating positive affirmations into the daily routine is simple and straightforward. They can be repeated first thing in the morning, as part of a daily meditation or visualization practice, or at any other time of day. It is important to choose affirmations that resonate with personal values and goals, and to repeat them with conviction and belief.

In addition to positive affirmations, there are other strategies for building self-esteem, including engaging in activities that promote a sense of accomplishment and success, seeking feedback and support from others, and practicing gratitude and self-compassion.

Building self-esteem through positive affirmations is a powerful strategy for increasing motivation and resilience. By incorporating these affirmations into the daily routine, individuals can cultivate feelings of self-worth, confidence, and motivation, and achieve their goals with greater ease and success. In the final chapter of this book, we will explore the importance of celebrating successes, staying motivated, and seeking support when needed, as key strategies for achieving and maintaining self-motivation and success.

"Success is not how high you have climbed, but how you make a positive difference to the world."

- Roy T. Bennett

ꕥ

VIII

The Power of Positive Thinking and Gratitude

Positive thinking and gratitude are powerful tools for increasing self-motivation and promoting success. By adopting a positive outlook and focusing on what is good in life, individuals can cultivate a growth mindset, overcome obstacles, and achieve their goals with greater ease and success. In this chapter, we will explore the importance of positive thinking and gratitude, and provide practical tips for incorporating these practices into daily life.

Positive thinking is the practice of focusing on the good in life, and avoiding negative thoughts and beliefs. It is a critical component of self-motivation, as negative thoughts and beliefs can undermine motivation, increase stress, and hinder progress towards goals. Positive thinking, on the other hand, has been shown to increase motivation, reduce stress, and improve overall well-being.

Gratitude is the practice of appreciating what is good in life, and focusing on the positive aspects of life experiences. It has been shown to increase feelings of happiness and well-being, and to reduce stress and anxiety. Furthermore, gratitude has been linked to increased motivation and resilience, as individuals who cultivate gratitude are less likely to give up in the face of challenges and obstacles.

Incorporating positive thinking and gratitude into the daily routine is simple and straightforward. Some strategies for promoting positive thinking and gratitude include:

Writing down three things to be grateful for each day

Practicing positive affirmations

Engaging in activities that promote feelings of happiness and well-being

Surrounding oneself with positive, supportive people

Practicing mindfulness and meditation

Positive thinking and gratitude are powerful tools for increasing self-motivation and promoting success. By incorporating these practices into daily life, individuals can cultivate a growth mindset, reduce stress and anxiety, and achieve their goals with greater ease and success. It is essential to remember that success is not just about achieving goals, but also about cultivating happiness and well-being in the journey towards those goals. By focusing on positive thinking and gratitude, individuals can cultivate a fulfilling and motivated life, and achieve success on all levels.

"Success is the sum of small efforts, repeated day in and day out."

- Robert Collier

ꟹ

IX

Dealing with Failure and Learning from Mistakes

Failure is an inevitable part of the journey towards success. No one succeeds without experiencing failure along the way. The difference between those who achieve their goals and those who do not is how they deal with failure and the lessons they learn from their mistakes. In this chapter, we will explore the importance of embracing failure and learning from mistakes, and provide practical tips for dealing with failure and turning it into a positive experience.

Embracing failure and learning from mistakes is critical for self-motivation and success. Failure can often be disheartening and deflating, and it is easy to become discouraged and give up on goals. However, it is important to understand that failure is not the end, but rather an opportunity to learn and grow. By embracing failure and learning from mistakes, individuals can build resilience, increase motivation, and achieve their goals with greater ease and success.

Learning from mistakes is a powerful tool for self-motivation. By examining what went wrong, individuals can identify areas for improvement, and make changes that will help them achieve their goals. Furthermore, learning from mistakes can increase self-confidence, as individuals come to understand that failure is not a reflection of their abilities, but rather an opportunity to learn and grow.

Incorporating a growth mindset and embracing failure into the daily routine is simple and straightforward. Some strategies for embracing failure and learning from mistakes include:

Embracing failure as an opportunity to learn and grow

Examining what went wrong and identifying areas for improvement

Reframing failure as a positive experience

Celebrating successes, no matter how small

Surrounding oneself with positive, supportive people

Embracing failure and learning from mistakes is critical for self-motivation and success. By embracing failure as an opportunity to learn and grow, individuals can build resilience, increase motivation, and achieve their goals with greater ease and success. It is essential to remember that success is not about avoiding failure, but rather about embracing it, learning from it, and using it as a tool for growth and improvement. By embracing failure and learning from mistakes, individuals can achieve their goals, and cultivate a fulfilling and motivated life.

"Success is not a destination, it's a journey."

- Zig Ziglar

ઇ

X

Building a Support System and Connecting with Others

Having a strong support system and connecting with others is a critical component of self-motivation and success. Having people in our lives who believe in us and support our goals can provide the encouragement and motivation we need to overcome challenges and reach our goals. In this chapter, we will explore the importance of building a support system and connecting with others, and provide practical tips for doing so.

Building a strong support system is essential for self-motivation and success. A supportive network of family, friends, and colleagues can provide encouragement, motivation, and a sounding board for ideas. When faced with obstacles or setbacks, having a support system in place can make all the difference in maintaining motivation and persevering towards our goals.

Connecting with others who share similar goals and interests is also an important part of building a supportive network. Joining clubs, organizations, or communities of like-minded individuals can provide a sense of belonging, and increase motivation and engagement in reaching our goals. In addition, connecting with others who have already achieved our goals can provide valuable insights and inspiration for our own journey.

There are several strategies for building a supportive network and connecting with others, including:

Surrounding oneself with positive, supportive people

Joining clubs, organizations, or communities of like-minded individuals

Building relationships with people who have already achieved our goals

Volunteering for causes or organizations that align with our values

Reaching out to friends, family, and colleagues for support

Building a strong support system and connecting with others is a critical component of self-motivation and success. Having a network of supportive people who believe in us and support our goals can provide the encouragement and motivation we need to overcome challenges and reach our goals. By building relationships with others who share similar goals and interests, and connecting with people who have already achieved our goals, individuals can cultivate a supportive and motivated community that will help them achieve their goals and live a fulfilling life.

"Success is the result of perfection, hard work, learning from failure, loyalty, and persistence."

- Colin Powell

ꕤ

XI

Finding and Pursuing Your Passions

Finding and pursuing our passions is a key factor in self-motivation and success. When we align our goals with our passions, we are more likely to be motivated, engaged, and fulfilled in our pursuits. In this chapter, we will explore the importance of finding and pursuing our passions, and provide practical tips for doing so.

Finding our passions is a process of self-discovery that involves exploring our interests, strengths, and values. This process can involve trying new things, reflecting on our experiences, and seeking out opportunities to pursue our passions. When we find our passions, we are able to tap into a source of energy, motivation, and inspiration that can drive us towards success.

Once we have found our passions, it is important to pursue them in a way that is aligned with our goals and values. This may involve setting goals and taking action to turn our passions into a fulfilling career, or engaging in activities that bring us joy and fulfillment. Pursuing our passions requires a commitment to self-motivation and personal growth, as well as a willingness to take risks and pursue our goals with determination and perseverance.

There are several strategies for finding and pursuing our passions, including:

Exploring our interests, strengths, and values

Trying new things and stepping outside our comfort zone

Seeking out opportunities to pursue our passions

Reflecting on our experiences and learning from failures

Taking action to turn our passions into a fulfilling career or personal fulfillment

Finding and pursuing our passions is a critical component of self-motivation and success. By aligning our goals with our passions, we are more likely to be motivated, engaged, and fulfilled in our pursuits. The process of finding our passions requires self-discovery, commitment, and perseverance, but the rewards are immeasurable. By tapping into our passions and pursuing them with determination, individuals can achieve success, find fulfillment, and lead a rich and fulfilling life.

"Success is the ability to go from one failure to another with no loss of enthusiasm."

- Winston S. Churchill

ࣻ

XII

Understanding and Managing Perfectionism

Perfectionism can be a double-edged sword in our pursuit of success. On one hand, it can drive us to set high standards and strive for excellence. On the other hand, it can hold us back by causing anxiety, stress, and self-doubt. In this chapter, we will explore the nature of perfectionism, its impact on self-motivation and success, and provide practical tips for managing it.

Perfectionism is often defined as a persistent drive to attain an ideal or flawless performance, often accompanied by an excessive concern with making mistakes. Perfectionists often set unrealistic standards for themselves and others, and are often highly critical of their own performance. Perfectionism can be a source of motivation, but it can also cause significant stress and anxiety, and interfere with our ability to take risks and pursue our goals.

Perfectionism can have a negative impact on self-motivation and success in several ways. For example, it can lead to procrastination, as perfectionists may avoid starting a task for fear of making mistakes. It can also lead to self-doubt, as perfectionists may feel that their efforts are never good enough. Perfectionism can also cause burnout, as perfectionists may push themselves to the point of exhaustion in their pursuit of excellence.

To manage perfectionism, it is important to recognize its impact on our lives and to develop strategies to reduce its negative effects. Some strategies for managing perfectionism include:

Setting realistic goals and standards

Focusing on progress, rather than perfection

Practicing self-compassion and self-care

Learning to accept and embrace failure as a learning opportunity

Cultivating a growth mindset and embracing challenges as opportunities for growth and development

Perfectionism can be both a source of motivation and a hindrance to success. By understanding the nature of perfectionism and its impact on self-motivation and success, individuals can learn to manage it effectively, reduce its negative effects, and achieve their goals with greater ease and fulfillment. By recognizing the value of progress and embracing the challenges of growth, individuals can find a healthy balance between striving for excellence and avoiding the pitfalls of perfectionism.

"Success is not final, failure is not fatal: it is the courage to continue that counts."

- Winston S. Churchill

ꕥ

XIII

Building Self-Compassion

Self-compassion is a critical component of self-motivation and success. It involves treating oneself with kindness, understanding, and compassion in the face of life's challenges and setbacks. In this chapter, we will explore the nature of self-compassion and its impact on self-motivation and success, and provide practical tips for building self-compassion.

Self-compassion is characterized by three core components: self-kindness, common humanity, and mindfulness. Self-kindness involves treating oneself with kindness and understanding, even in the face of failure or mistakes. Common humanity involves recognizing that suffering and difficulties are part of the human experience, and that we are not alone in our struggles. Mindfulness involves a non-judgmental awareness of our experiences in the present moment.

Self-compassion has been shown to have a positive impact on well-being, motivation, and success. For example, self-compassion has been associated with greater resilience, lower levels of anxiety and depression, and improved motivation and performance.

To build self-compassion, individuals can practice several strategies, including:

Practicing self-kindness and self-care, such as taking breaks, engaging in enjoyable activities, and treating oneself with kindness and understanding

Engaging in mindfulness and self-reflection, such as journaling, meditation, or other forms of introspection

Cultivating a growth mindset and embracing challenges as opportunities for growth and development

Practicing self-compassionate self-talk, such as speaking to oneself with kindness and understanding, rather than criticism and self-doubt

Self-compassion is a critical component of self-motivation and success. By treating oneself with kindness and understanding, and recognizing that life's challenges and setbacks are a part of the human experience, individuals can develop greater resilience, motivation, and success. By embracing self-compassion, individuals can cultivate a supportive inner voice, build greater self-awareness, and find the strength to pursue their goals with greater ease and fulfillment.

"Success is not a matter of luck, but of preparation and hard work."

- Mark Twain

ꕤ

XIV

The Role of Mindfulness in Self-Motivation

Self-motivation is the key to achieving your goals and reaching success. But, what many people don't realize is that mindfulness plays a crucial role in the equation. Mindfulness refers to the practice of being present in the moment and focusing on the here and now. It involves paying attention to your thoughts, feelings, and sensations in a non-judgmental way. By incorporating mindfulness into your daily routine, you can improve your self-motivation and achieve greater success in all areas of your life.

One of the main benefits of mindfulness is that it helps you to reduce stress and anxiety. When you are under stress, it can be difficult to stay focused and motivated. The negative thoughts and emotions that come with stress can interfere with your ability to concentrate and get things done. By practicing mindfulness, you can learn to become more aware of your thoughts and emotions and respond to them in a calm and centered way. This, in turn, can help you to reduce stress and maintain your motivation levels, even when you are faced with challenges and setbacks.

Another benefit of mindfulness is that it helps you to cultivate greater self-awareness. When you are mindful, you are more in tune with your thoughts and emotions, which allows you to better understand what drives your behavior. This can help you to identify any limiting beliefs or negative thought patterns that may be holding you back from reaching your goals. By learning to become more self-aware, you can start to challenge these beliefs and develop new, more positive and empowering ways of thinking.

Mindfulness also helps you to cultivate a positive attitude. By focusing on the present moment and becoming more aware of your thoughts and emotions, you can start to recognize when you are engaging in negative self-talk or dwelling on past failures. This, in turn, can help you to shift your focus to the present and cultivate a more positive outlook. With a positive attitude, you are more likely to be motivated and focused on reaching your goals.

Finally, mindfulness can also help you to increase your level of self-compassion. Self-compassion refers to the ability to be kind and understanding to yourself when things don't go as planned. When you are mindful, you are more aware of your thoughts and feelings, which can help you to recognize when you are being too hard on yourself. By practicing self-compassion, you can start to develop a more nurturing and supportive inner dialogue, which will help you to stay motivated and focused on reaching your goals.

Mindfulness is an important tool in the pursuit of self-motivation and success. By incorporating mindfulness into your daily routine, you can reduce stress and anxiety, cultivate self-awareness, develop a positive attitude, and increase your level of self-compassion. With these benefits, you will be better equipped to stay motivated and focused on reaching your goals, no matter what challenges you may face along the way.

"Success is not just about what you accomplish in your life, it's about what you inspire others to do."

ꕥ

XV

Putting it All Together and Reaching Your Goals with Self-Motivation

In this book, we have explored the various strategies and techniques that can help you motivate yourself to reach your goals. From understanding the importance of self-motivation to finding and pursuing your passions, and from building resilience to managing negative emotions, we have covered a range of topics that can help you stay motivated and achieve your desired outcomes.

In order to be successful in reaching your goals, it is essential that you apply these strategies in a holistic and consistent manner. Self-motivation is not something that can be achieved overnight, but rather it is a continuous process of self-reflection, self-improvement, and growth.

To begin with, you should take a step back and reflect on your current habits and thought patterns. Take note of what works for you and what doesn't, and start making small, incremental changes to your daily routine that will help you build self-motivation over time.

Next, create a plan for reaching your goals that is specific, measurable, achievable, relevant, and time-bound. Set achievable and realistic goals for yourself, and break them down into smaller, manageable steps. Having a plan in place will help you stay focused and motivated, and ensure that you are making progress towards your desired outcomes.

Along the way, be mindful of your thoughts and emotions, and work on building mental and physical resilience. Use positive affirmations to build self-esteem and self-compassion, and practice mindfulness to stay focused and grounded. Surround yourself with a supportive network of friends and family, and seek help and advice when you need it.

Finally, remember that setbacks and failures are a normal part of the journey towards success. Don't be too hard on yourself, and use your mistakes as opportunities to learn and grow. Celebrate your successes, no matter how small, and stay motivated and focused on your goals.

Self-motivation is a powerful tool for achieving success. By applying the strategies and techniques outlined in this book, you can develop the motivation and resilience needed to overcome obstacles and reach your goals. So take control of your life and start your journey towards self-motivated success today!

"Success is a state of mind. If you want success, start thinking of yourself as a success."

- Joyce Brothers

ꟸ

Other Books Of The Author

1. The Moments When I Met God
2. Kashiyile Theertha Pathangal
3. GURU GYAN VANI
4. Abhiprerak Gita
5. ASSI SE JAIN GHAT TAK
6. Hopelessness of Arjuna
7. The Soul and It's True Nature
8. Sense of Action (Karma)
9. Action through Wisdom
10. Action through Wisdom
11. THEORY AND PRACTICAL OF EVERY ACTION
12. LOGICAL UNDERSTANDING OF THE SUPREME
13. THE IMPERISHABLE SUPREME
14. Yatra Nishadraj se Hanuman Ghat Tak
15. Yatra Karnatak Ghat se Raja Ghat Tak
16. Yatra Pandey Ghat se Prayagraj Ghat Tak
17. Yatra Ranjendra Prasad Ghat se Dattatreya Ghat Tak
18. YaatraSindhiya Ghat se Gwaliar Ghat Tak
19. Yatra Mangala Gauri Ghat se Hanuman Gadhi Ghat Tak
20. Yatra Gaay Ghat Se Nishad Ghat Tak
21. MAA GANGA, GHATEN EVM UTSAV
22. Ganga Arti Dev Deepavali evam Any Utsav
23. Potentials of Digitalized India
24. VEDIC CONSCIOUSNESS
25. A Brief Introduction to Vedic Science
26. Kashi ke Barah Jyotirling
27. IMPACT OF MOTIVATION
28. Let's have a Milky Way Journey
29. Color Therapy in a Nutshell

30. Rigveda in a Nutshell
31. Yajurveda in a Nutshell
32. Samveda in a Nutshell
33. Atharva Veda in a Nutshell
34. Ayushman Bhava - Ayurveda
35. Srimad Bhagavad Gita and Upanishad Connection
36. Srimad Bhagavad Gita - an attempt to summarize each chapter.
37. Facts and Impact of Nakshatra
38. Astro Gems - NAVARATNA
39. Ekadashi - A Concise Overview
40. A Concise View of Hanuman Chalisa
41. Inspirational Gita
42. Nakshatraranyam
43. Summary of 18 Mahapuranas
44. Synopsis of 18 Upa Puranas
45. Rigvediya Upanishads
46. Shukla Yajurvediya Upanishads
47. Krishna Yajurvediya Upanishads
48. Samavediya Upanishads
49. Atharvavediya Upanishads
50. The Seven Great Sages
51. From Rocket Scientist to President Dr. APJ Abdul Kalam
52. The Visionary's Voice - Quotes of Dr. APJ Abdul Kalam
53. The Wisdom of Swami Vivekananda: Insights and Inspiration from a Legendary Spiritual Teacher
54. Ayurvedic Remedies from the Garden
55. Sages and Seers
56. Rising Strong – Motivational Stories of Women
57. Beyond Flames -Mystery stories of Funeral Ghat Manikarnika
58. The Origins of Tulsi: A Look at the Mythological Roots of the Plant"

59. The Holistic Cow: A Look at the Physical, Spiritual, and Cultural Importance of Cows in India
60. Arts of Healing
61. Exploring the Divine
62. Understanding Five Elements
63. The Etymology of Ram
64. Symbols of India
65. Voice of Change (About Speeches of Great Men)
66. She Speaks (About Speeches of Great Women)
67. Patriotism on Celluloid – Brief About Patriotic Films
68. The Music of Motivation: A Brief Guide to Inspirational Film Songs
69. **Unlocking the Secrets of the Dashopanishads**
70. A Cultural Mosaic
71. Ancient Traditions, Modern Minds
72. Ecos of Ancient Wisdom
73. Beneath the Surface
74. From Temples to Ashrams
75. Sages of the Subcontinent
76. The Art of Healling (Ayurveda, Yoga & Naturopathy)
77. Indian Kitchen
78. The Festivals of India
79. The Indian Epics Retold
80. The Power of Mantras
81. The Indian River Ganges
82. The Indian Architecture
83. Rites of Passage
84. The Indian Silk Road
85. The Indian Literature
86. The Indian Villages
87. The Indian Folks & Crafts
88. The Way of Buddha
89. The Ramayan of Tulsidas

90. Astrological Remedies
91. The Secret Power of Motivation
92. Secret of Developing your Inner Strength
93. The Secret Path to Motivation
94. The Art and Secret of Positive Thinking
95. The Secrets of Practicing Ethical Living
96. Indian Art and Painting
97. The Indian Herbalism
98. Bharatanatyam to Kathak
99. Exploring India's Astrological Remedies
100. The Indian Festival of Flowers
101. Indian Handicrafts
102. The Splashes of Joy – India's Colour Festival
103. The Indian Science of Astrology
104. The Indian Mythology
105. Path to Enlightenment
106. The Indian Spirituality for Children
107. Aromas of India
108. The Secrets of Healthy Relationships
109. Ancestral Ties
110. The Indian Street Food
111. Discovering America
112. The Indian Textile
113. Listening to Motivational Speeches
114. Taste of India
115. A Cultural Journey through Indian Nuptials
116. Motivational Quote for Change
117. Secret Strategies for Making Money
118. Secrets to Cultivate a Positive Mindset
119. A Tapestry of Cultures: Exploring India from Kashmir to Kanyakumari
120. Achieving Your Dreams with Resilience: Secret Strategies for Overcoming Obstacles

121. Innovative Startups - 25 Startup Ideas to Spark Your Business Creativity
122. Export Management: Strategies for Global Success
123. Exporting from India - A Step by Step Guide
124. Finance Fundamentals: Mastering Financial Management for Business Success
125. Global Growth Strategies for International Business Development
126. Marketing Mastery: Unlocking the Secrets of Modern Marketing
127. Operations Mastery: Managing the Flow of Value in Business
128. Strategic Business Management: Navigating the Modern Business Landscape
129. Human Resource Management Strategies for Building and Managing a High Performance Team
130. The Indian Landscapes and Nature: An Exploration Of India's Natural Beauty And Diversity
131. The Indian Street Performances: A Cultural Exploration of India's Street Performances
132. Affirming Your Self-Worth: Strategies for Achieving Emotional Wellbeing
133. Cultivating Self-Discipline: Secrets Methods for Achieving Your Goals
134. Embracing Change: Strategies for Adapting to Life's Challenges
135. Embracing Your Uniqueness: Secret Strategies for Living an Authentic Life
136. Finding Motivation in Despondency: Coping with Difficult Times
137. Embracing Change
138. Learning to Love Yourself
139. Managing Time for Yourself

140. Unlock the keys to Self-Motivation
141. Secret to Boost Confidence
142. Unlocking your Potential: A Path to Inner-strength & Success
143. Secrets to Develop Authentic Relationship
144. Secrets to Build a Successful Career
145. Secrets to Live with Gratitude
146. Secrets to Create a Life of Abundance
147. Secrets to Cultivate Self-Awareness
148. The Power of Helping Hands
149. Finding Your Passion
150. The Indian Mythical Creatures
151. The Indian Women Saints
152. The Wisdom of the Saints
153. "The Indian Royalty: A Cultural and Historical Exploration of India's Maharajas and their kingdom"
154. The Mystic Land: A Cultural and Spiritual Exploration of India"
155. India's Spiritual Legacy – Discovering the Cultural and Religious Significance of Bhakti Yoga.
156. The Indian Folktales: An Exploration of India's Oral Folklore Traditions
157. Steeping In History: A Look at India's Iconic Tea Culture
158. The Indian Way Of Life: An Exploration Of The Philosophy And Practices Of Indian Culture
159. From Silence to Sound: A Cultural and Historical Study of Indian Cinema
160. Chronicles of Indian Style: Tracing the Transformations of Traditional and Contemporary Fashion
161. Decorating India: A Journey Through the Traditions and Transformations of Home Design
162. Adornments of India: A Journey Through the History and Artistry Behind Indian Jewelry

163. The Indian Royal Kitchens: A Gastronomic Journey Through the Kitchens of India's Maharajas
164. The Indian Sports: An Insight into the History and Significance of Indian Traditional Sports
165. The Indian Traditional Games: A Study Of The Significance And Evolution Of Indian Traditional Games
166. Secrets to Make Positive Choices: Strategies for Achieving Your Goals
167. Secrets to Motivate Yourself for Success Strategies for Reaching Your Goals

CONTACT

DR. JAGADEESH PILLAI

MBA & PhD in Vedic Science

Four Times Guinness World Record Holder

Winner of Mahatma Gandhi Vishwa Shanti Puraskar and Global Peace Ambassador

Gemology, Astro & Vastu Consultant - Spiritual Counselor

Consultant for designing World Record Ideas

Efficient Tarot Card Reader

9839093003

myrichindia@gmail.com

drjagadeeshpillai@facebook

drjagadeeshpillai@instagram
jagadeeshpillai@youtube

www. JAGADEESHPILLAI.com

|| LOKAHA SAMASTHAHA SUKHINO BHAVANTU ||

9 798889 597957

Printed by Libri Plureos GmbH in Hamburg,
Germany